12/08   W9-BKF-326

Fact Finders®

MEDIA LITERACY

What's Your Source?

Questioning the News

by Stergios Botzakis

Capstone press®

Mankato, Minnesota

Fact Finders are published by Capstone Press,
151 Good Counsel Drive, P.O. Box 669, Mankato, Minnesota 56002.
www.capstonepress.com

Library of Congress Cataloging-in-Publication Data
Botzakis, Stergios.
    What's your source? : questioning the news / Stergios Botzakis.
    p. cm. — (Fact Finders. Media literacy)
    Includes bibliographical references and index.
    Summary: "Describes what media is, how the news is a part of media, and encourages
readers to question the medium's influential messages" — Provided by publisher.
    ISBN-13: 978-1-4296-1992-9 (hardcover)
    ISBN-10: 1-4296-1992-9 (hardcover)
    1. Journalism — Objectivity — Juvenile literature. 2. Journalism — Juvenile literature.
I. Title. II. Series.
PN4784.O24B69 2009
302.23 — dc22   2007050515

Editorial Credits

Jennifer Besel, editor; Juliette Peters, set designer; Kyle Grenz, book designer;
    Jo Miller, photo researcher

Photo Credits

All photos by Capstone Press, except:
AP Images/Byron Rollins, 18
Courtesy of Stergios Botzakis, 32
Getty Images Inc./AFP/Doug Collier, 19 (Jewell)
Landov LLC/CBS, 28 (right)
Shutterstock/A.S. Zain, 9 (bottom); Guy Erwood, 19, 21 (background)

1 2 3 4 5 6 13 12 11 10 09 08

TABLE OF CONTENTS

News Discovered Everywhere

Did you have reporters on your lawn this morning? Probably not. Most people aren't followed by paparazzi. But we are all surrounded by news coverage. It's on TV, on the radio, in newspapers, and even on the Internet.

The **media** is a part of our daily lives. And a big part of the media is the news. We learn about major events, sports, weather, and entertainment from the news.

The news gives us information about the world around us. But the news can also **influence** us. The way news is presented can change how we think or feel. But it doesn't have to. Here are a few questions to ask yourself the next time you watch or read the news.

QUESTION IT!

Who made the message and why?

Who is the message for?

How might others view the message differently?

What is left out of the message?

How does the message get and keep my attention?

Deliver News, Make Money

Who made the message and why?

Long ago, people didn't hear about a news event until days or weeks after it happened. News spread slowly from one part of the world to another. People had to bring newspapers across the ocean.

But that is no longer true today. Inventions like radio, television, and the Internet make it possible to get news as soon as it happens. News companies use these inventions to get us information fast.

News can be posted on the Internet as fast as a person can type. When world leaders die, we learn about it within seconds.

Making Money

But the companies that put out the news also have another purpose. They want to make money. You see, news companies have more than just news. They have a way to reach a lot of people. Radio and TV stations sell airtime to **advertisers**. Advertisers pay money to play their commercials during news programs. Web sites, magazines, and newspapers sell ad space. That's why there are ads on MSNBC.com and in *Newsweek*.

Do you think ads that appear online or in magazines influence you?

Many people help bring you the news. Here are some of the key players.

The **JOURNALIST** does research about news stories and reports the news.

The **PHOTOGRAPHER** is also at the news scene. Photographers take photos or video to tell the story.

The **EDITOR** checks the facts for each news report. Editors work in different departments, such as sports or fashion.

The **NEWS DIRECTOR** decides which stories to use for the news.

The **ANALYST** gives an opinion about a news story. This person is often entertaining or has some special knowledge about a story.

The **NEWSWIRES** are big agencies that have journalists all over the world. They sell stories to news outlets that don't have money to send reporters around the world.

Audience Targeted During News

Who is the message for?

News outlets don't have time or space to tell you about every news event. How do they know what news matters to you? They do lots and lots of research. TV stations study Nielsen ratings. These scores tell how many people have news programs on and when. Nielsen research also tells who is watching, based on age and gender. Radio stations get the same kind of information from Arbitron ratings. This information helps news companies decide what stories appeal to their target audiences. News companies need to attract their audiences. It's the only way they can keep advertisers paying for airtime.

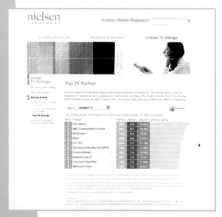

All the News That's Fit to Print

Most magazines and newspapers have Web versions. They use online resources to track their audiences. It is easy to see which stories are visited most online. Publishers keep track of these page views with hit counters. If a certain story is popular, they'll probably keep reporting on it. And you'll probably see similar stories in the future.

In 2007, news outlets filled their pages and newscasts with information about Anna Nicole Smith's death. This may not have been the most important news in the world. But companies reported on it because their target audiences were interested.

News for Everyone

News comes in lots of forms. Each version targets a specific audience. Some news sources are meant for certain age groups. News stories on CNN will be very different from ones on Channel One. CNN is aimed at adults. Channel One is for kids. You don't see a lot of extreme skateboarders on news networks targeting adults.

Channel One

People like to get their news in different ways. Media outlets try to meet these needs. Take a look at the many ways to get news on TV. Shows called newsmagazines offer fewer stories and more details. You'll find short looped stories on 24-hour news channels. Other channels broadcast local news. And that's just TV. Newspapers, magazines, and radio offer hundreds of other options. There's a news outlet for every audience.

Values Found to Affect Thoughts

How might others view this message differently?

Let's say you're in school and a boy was tipping his chair back. He tips back too far and lands with a huge CRASH! You and your friends worry about the boy. Some of your other classmates think this is hilarious. To the teacher, it is scary. Events create different feelings in different people. And each person will tell this piece of news differently. A person's values, or beliefs, affect how he or she feels about news stories. Your age, gender, or even religious beliefs affect how you think about an event.

These two papers are reporting on the same event. But the headlines focus on different parts of the story. Do you think the reporters' values influenced what they focused on?

High School Herald
Senior boy crashes to floor
Students laugh

Classroom Chronicle
Student falls to floor after chair accident
Fellow students worry about his health

Variable Values

News reporters have their own values too. Reporters should try to give fair reports on events. But their values play a big part in how they talk about stories. That's why every reporter focuses on different details.

Newspapers cover similar stories, but they target the information to fit their audience's values. One paper talks about the behind-the-scenes effects of an international money issue. Another paper covers the day-to-day changes in the markets.

TRY IT OUT!

Next time you are at a dance or a game, pay attention to what goes on. Afterward, talk with some friends who were also there. Trade stories and see what everyone noticed. Make a list of the stories. Even though you were at the same event, you might be surprised by the different stories you report.

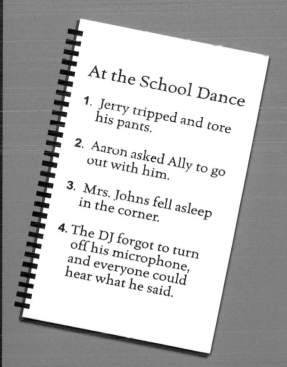

At the School Dance

1. Jerry tripped and tore his pants.

2. Aaron asked Ally to go out with him.

3. Mrs. Johns fell asleep in the corner.

4. The DJ forgot to turn off his microphone, and everyone could hear what he said.

15

Unfair News Reports

Have you ever looked at a cheerleader and assumed she was dumb? Or have you ever called the smart kid a nerd? These assumptions are called **stereotypes**. And a stereotype never tells you the real story about a person. The cheerleader might have straight As. The smart kid could be an amazing basketball player.

Stereotypes find their way into news stories too. Often African Americans are shown as criminals. Muslims are often shown as terrorists. The problem is that the news is only focusing on the actions of a few people. Most African Americans and Muslims are not criminals. But if you don't question what you see, you wouldn't know that. Next time you watch the news, think about how someone else would view the story.

This picture was included in a story about Muslims protesting an offensive cartoon. Do you think this picture shows the person in a fair way?

Can You Spot the Stereotype?

A story can be told many ways. Reporters choose which details to include and which to leave out. When stereotypes creep into a story, the news focuses on the people rather than the events. Below are four different versions of the same news event. Which report is the most fair and balanced? Can you spot the stereotypes?

1. Three high school students have been accused of shooting a woman in a local neighborhood.

2. Three Mexican high school students have been accused of shooting a woman in a local neighborhood.

3. Three high school students were involved in the shooting of a woman in a local neighborhood. Neighbors in the area told police the students tried to help a woman who was being held at gunpoint. The woman was shot when the students tried to free her.

4. Three Mexican high school students have been accused of shooting a woman in Phoenix, Arizona. The woman was a competitor in the Miss Arizona pageant.

What is left out of the message?

Sometimes news people jump to conclusions when they race to break stories. One of the most famous examples of this happened in 1948. President Harry S. Truman was running for reelection against Thomas Dewey. Early election results showed Dewey was ahead. But counting the votes took time. The *Chicago Daily Tribune* wanted to announce the results before anyone else. They printed their paper before all the votes were counted. They printed that Dewey had won. But he didn't win. Truman won, and the paper had printed the wrong headline.

LINGO
break: to report a story first

President Harry S. Truman

Reality Check

Bad information or rushes to judgment can ruin a person's life. Richard Jewell was a security guard who alerted police to a bomb at the 1996 Summer Olympics in Atlanta. His actions saved many people's lives. But for a time, the FBI thought Jewell made the bomb. This made for a juicy news story. Many news channels and papers said Jewell was guilty. Eventually, it came out that Jewell was a hero, but his reputation was still badly damaged.

Richard Jewell

Picking Favorites

When you fight with your brother, you might think your parents pick his side over yours. They might have a **bias**. In the news business, some reporters pick sides too. News people tend to favor politicians they agree with. But they can also make people they don't agree with seem worse.

Reporters should not favor one side of a story over another. If you see or hear that happening in a story, stop and think. Do you feel the same way? You can also check other news outlets to see how they report the story. You might find that some reporters leave out bits of information. And that missing information could change the meaning of the story.

Check the coverage of a story online and in newspapers. See if they report the same details or if they have different information.

Reality Check

The Sinclair Broadcast Group owns eight TV stations that show ABC's programming. In 2004, the Sinclair Broadcast Group decided not to show the April 30 edition of *Nightline*. On that day's show, reporters read the names of all the U.S. soldiers who had died in Iraq since 2003. The Sinclair Broadcast Group felt the news show was doing this to make the war seem like a bad idea. The people at *Nightline* said they were doing it to honor soldiers.

Censorship by corporations that control the news is a big issue. Do you think a corporation would let reporters talk about a story that would be bad for the company?

Worrisome Reports

News outlets want to report exciting stories. To do so, they sometimes make stories sound crazier than they are. In 2007, Andrew Speaker rode on an airplane while he was sick with tuberculosis. News people reported the story, saying he was highly contagious. This made many people worried about their safety while traveling. It turned out that Speaker's disease was not highly contagious. The story quickly went away when it wasn't as bad as the news had made it out to be.

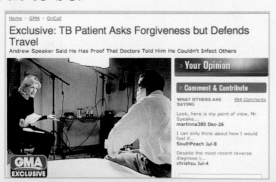

Home > GMA > OnCall

Exclusive: TB Patient Asks Forgiveness but Defends Travel
Andrew Speaker Said He Has Proof That Doctors Told Him He Couldn't Infect Others

► **Your Opinion**

► **Comment & Contribute**

WHAT OTHERS ARE SAYING · 954 Comments

Look, here is my point of view, Mr. Speake...
martinna380 Dec-26

I can only think about how I would feel if...
SouthPeach Jul-8

Despite the most recent reverse diagnose t...
chrishsu Jul-4

TRY IT OUT!

Pretend you're a reporter. Your assignment is to write a story about your best friend's life. But you have to do it with only 500 words. Make a list of details you will include in your story.

- Will you include embarrassing stories about your friend?

- Will you include information about times your friend got in trouble?

Remember, leaving out information always changes the real story in some way.

My Best Friend, Suzie

Suzie was born on May 17. She likes to ride bike, read, and play board games. She also likes to ice skate. One time Suzie was skating and she lost her balance. She fell down right in front of the judges.

A Note about Sources

Where did the reporter get his or her information? That's a great question to ask when you're learning about a news story. The **sources** reporters use to get information should be reliable. The more reliable their sources, the more we can trust the report.

Say you're reading an article in the paper about dangerous snakes. You read, "According to Tom Smith, a man who likes reptiles, garter snakes are poisonous." Now let's say you read a magazine article about the same topic. You read, "According to Dr. Lance Jones, biologist at New York University, garter snakes are not poisonous." Which source is the most reliable?

There are many ways to check facts. Online databases or encyclopedias are helpful. Talking with experts is also a good way to gather information.

Fires, War Attract Viewers

How does the message get and keep my attention?

News outlets have to get your attention fast. They often run stories about dangerous things like fires, disasters, crime, and war. Newspapers and Web sites use punchy headlines to attract readers. TV and radio stations use sound bites to communicate information quickly.

Many news sources use graphics to jazz up their stories. Graphics on TV help tell the story. Footage of the Iraq war often includes a fancy graphic and title, such as "Operation: Enduring Freedom." That gets viewers' attention.

Do you think fancy graphics or powerful color photographs get your attention?

Celebrity News

News sources often use celebrity stories to attract viewers. Just think of how much attention gets paid to the troubles of Britney Spears and Paris Hilton. News outlets reported more than 1,000 different stories about Paris alone in 2007. These stories ranged from what clothes she wore to updates about her dog. Do these stories grab your interest?

LINGO

sound bite: a quick, catchy comment said by a public figure that news outlets play in a broadcast

Exclusive!

News people use many tricks to keep us coming back for more. You might have heard some of these before.

YOU HEARD IT HERE FIRST!

News channels compete with each other to break stories first. They want you to know that they will get you the news faster and better than anyone else.

COMING UP . . .

News people use teasers to let you know what's coming up. They use stories that hit close to home, such as toy recalls or health warnings, to keep viewers watching.

LINGO

teaser: a statement made by a news anchor to get us interested in what's coming next

THE MOST TRUSTED NEWS SOURCE!

News stations want you to know that they get the stories right. They send the message that you can count on them to tell you the truth.

ON THE SCENE!

News channels take pride in being places when news stories happen. This is why some unlucky reporter is always standing outside in a hurricane.

Signing Off

News people work hard to keep us informed. But you still need to ask questions to help make sense of all the information you get. So grab that newspaper, and have some fun questioning the news around you!

Time Line

The first regularly published newspaper is printed in Germany.

CBS radio does a report with journalists located around the world for the first time on a daily national broadcast.

1609 **1846** **1938** **1948**

The Associated Press newswire is formed.

AP Associated Press

CBS-TV News begins. It is the first regularly scheduled television news program.

Sinclair Broadcast
Group blocks the April 30
edition of ABC's *Nightline*
from playing on the
company's TV stations.
Many people protest the
decision as censorship.

CNN, the first
24-hour news station,
begins broadcasting.

2004

1996

1980

News outlets report that
Richard Jewell is guilty
of making the bomb at
the Summer Olympics.
He is later cleared, but
the news reports hurt
his reputation.

GLOSSARY

advertiser (AD-ver-tize-uhr) — a company that pays money to sell its product during the news

bias (BYE-uhs) — favoring one person or point of view over another

censorship (SEN-suhr-ship) — the removal of something that is thought to be harmful or offensive to the public

influence (IN-floo-uhnss) — to have an effect on someone or something

media (MEE-dee-uh) — a group of mediums that communicates messages; one piece of the media, like the news, is called a medium.

source (SORSS) — someone or something that provides information

stereotype (STER-ee-oh-tipe) — an overly simple opinion of a person, group, or thing

INTERNET SITES

FactHound offers a safe, fun way to find Internet sites related to this book. All of the sites on FactHound have been researched by our staff.

Here's how:

1. Visit *www.facthound.com*

2. Choose your grade level.

3. Type in this book ID **1429619929** for age-appropriate sites. You may also browse subjects by clicking on letters, or by clicking on pictures and words.

4. Click on the **Fetch It** button.

FactHound will fetch the best sites for you!

READ MORE

Ali, Dominic. *Media Madness: An Insider's Guide to Media*. Tonawanda, N.Y.: Kids Can Press, 2005.

Streissguth, Tom. *Media Bias*. Open For Debate. New York: Marshall Cavendish Benchmark, 2007.

INDEX

MEET THE AUTHOR

Stergios Botzakis has been interested in media his whole life. He has done much research on media, including how to use comic books and magazines in the classroom. He has presented his work at several national conferences, including the National Media Education Conference. Currently, Sterg teaches literacy education at the University of Tennessee.